Sir John A. Macdonald
The rascal who built Canada

Written by Jacqueline A. Brown
Illustrated by Suzanne Mogensen

Photo Credits
JackFruit Press Ltd would like to thank the Canadian National Archives for images appearing on pages 6 (E-00001790 Sir John A Macdonald Papers), 13 (C-95155), 16 (C-148218 © Confederation Life/Rogers Inc.), 31 (PA-146823), 32 (C-003693) and the reproduction of the campaign poster (C-006536) used on pages 35, 43 and the back cover. Louis Riel's coat on page 25 appears courtesy of © Canadian Museum of Civilization, catalogue no. E-111, photo Steven Darby and the photograph of 19th century school room (page 11) comes courtesy of the Sesquicentennial Museum and Archives, Toronto District School Board. Thank you to Getty Images for photographs appearing on page 3 (Burke/Triolo Productions), 9 (Photodisc Collection) and page 21 (Haywood Magee), to the Western Canada Pictorial Index for the photograph on page 33 and to Hagit Hadaya for taking the photograph of Isabella Clark Macdonald's tombstone, reproduced on page 19.

Publisher - Jacqueline Brown
Editor - Kaitlyn Hayes
Designer and Art Director – Marcel Lafleur
Researchers - Barbara Baillargeon and Peter Konieczny

JackFruit Press Ltd.
Toronto, Canada
www.jackfruitpress.com

National Library of Canada Cataloguing in Publication Data

Brown, Jacqueline, 1965-
Sir John A. Macdonald: the rascal who built Canada / Jacqueline Brown;
illustrator, Suzanne Mogensen.

Canada's Prime Ministers,
warts and all ; 1) Includes index.
ISBN 0-9736406-0-X

1. Macdonald, John A. (John Alexander), Sir, 1815-1891.
2. Prime ministers – Canada – Biography – Juvenile literature.
3. Canada – Politics and government – 1867-1896 – Juvenile literature.
I. Mogensen, Suzanne II. Title.
III. Series.
FC521.M3B76 2005
j971.05'1'092
C2004-906467-3

Printed and Bound in Canada

...So, I'm here to show you around this really cool series of books on great Canadians...

This book tells the story of Sir John A. Macdonald, Canada's first prime minister.

John was a man who had a lot of problems. But he overcame them. And he built this country! How cool is that?

Contents

Colourful, charismatic, and controversial 4

From rags to riches...
to rags again 8

The legal eagle becomes
a political powerhouse 12

Troubles and triumphs
in John's personal life 18

The new dominion
is threatened 24

Down, but not out 30

Exciting times in the making of a great country 36

Sir John: the man who dreamed
and schemed a country 38

Timeline:
The life and times of John A. Macdonald 40

Glossary:
Words and facts you might want to know 44

Index:
Where to find stuff in this book 48

What are these two objects and how were they used during John A's life? See page 11 for the answer.

This face should be very familiar to any Canadian. It appears on Canada's $10 bill. Most people assume that Canada was meant to be. But Canada might not have come into being without Sir John A. Macdonald's vision and determination.

Colourful, controversial, and charismatic

People called him a "frightful old rascal" and "the father and founder of this country." To this day, he is the only Prime Minister to throw up in the **House of Commons**, resign for dishonourable behaviour, and take up arms against invading Americans. He built a country and he built a railroad to cross it from coast to coast, but all his searching could not find a doctor to save the life of his invalid wife. Crowds went crazy with applause listening to him, newspapers reported his mad drunken bouts, and experts said he was nuts for adoring his daughter because she had a disability. When **Sir John Thompson**, Canada's fourth Prime Minister, was asked his opinion of Sir John A. Macdonald, he replied, "there is not one of us who had not lost his heart to him."

Want to know more? The words **in bold** are explained in the glossary at the back of the book.

A time before Canada existed

What does it mean to build a nation? Most people living today assume that Canada was meant to be because they cannot remember anything else. But don't kid yourself! Canada might not have happened at all. When Sir John A. Macdonald was a child, there was no vast, united country called Canada. Can you imagine a time when our provinces (called **colonies** in those days) argued about whether they should join the United States of America or remain British colonies forever? Can you imagine a time when the provinces fought so much with each other that lots of people didn't believe they could ever join together to create their own country? A time when most people didn't even believe that it was possible to build a railroad connecting eastern Canada with British Columbia, or that French- and English-speaking peoples could share a nation? But Sir John believed. And he worked his whole life long to make this dream of a strong, free, and just country named Canada come true.

Sir John followed his dream through some of the most exciting yet troubling events in Canada's history: the **Red River Rebellion**, the **Pacific Scandal**, the **Northwest Rebellion**, and the execution of **Louis Riel**. His personal life was just as challenging: lifelong financial difficulties, **alcoholism**, and the early deaths of his first wife and son. He made plenty of mistakes, learned from them, and kept on going forward. He was a charismatic and wise man whose legacy includes the Canadian Pacific Railway (CPR), the Royal Canadian Mounted Police (the RCMP, often called the Mounties), our first national park, and most importantly, Canada itself! He was the first Prime Minister of Canada and a man just as fascinating and diverse as the country he founded.

Tall and handsome with curly black hair and striking blue eyes, Sir John had a charming personality and winning ways. A magnetic speaker who loved having lots of people around him, he gave his first speech at age 6! His memory was incredible: he always remembered names, faces, and all the details of conversations. This made everyone who knew him feel important to him, and even people he had met only once or twice felt that he liked and respected them. As you can guess, this skill made him very popular. It was no surprise he rose to a leadership position in every group he joined!

REPORT

Of Resolutions adopted at a Conference of Delegates from the Provinces of Canada, Nova Scotia, and New Brunswick, and the Colonies of Newfoundland and Prince Edward Island, held at the City of Quebec, 10th October, 1864, as the Basis of a proposed Confederation of those Provinces and Colonies.

Quebec Conference Resolutions: This document, which is stored at the National Archives in Ottawa, led to the creation of Canada. Sir John's notes and doodles appear on its pages.

A charismatic personality

Sir John was highly intelligent and an excellent organizer. He was particularly talented at convincing other people to work with him to get things done. He often used his fabulous sense of humour to break through tension and help people get along with each other. He was the main author of the **British North America (BNA) Act**, which later became the Canadian **Constitution**. Imagine creating a document that would become the foundation of a country!

On the other hand, Sir John was, as they would say in those days, a rascal and a scalawag. He would do anything to make sure he got his own way… and he drank way too much whiskey. They nicknamed him "Old Tomorrow" because he was always putting difficult decisions off "until tomorrow," perhaps in the hopes that they would disappear. But with characteristic humour and charm, Sir John openly acknowledged his faults and just kept doing his best, saying, "As far as I am concerned, I've gone through life with one principle: 'Be to our faults a little blind, and to our virtues always kind.'"

So what does all this tell us about Sir John A. Macdonald? That he was a real person just like the rest of us – someone with talents and faults, whose vision led him and whose ambition sometimes misled him, who triumphed over personal difficulty at the same time as he struggled under it. While his life was seldom easy, it was always interesting!

There is a lot of prejudice against people with disabilities. But John ignores people's nasty comments and spends as much time as he can with his daughter, Mary. He often takes her to see him at work in the House of Commons.

1820

Figuring that his chances will be better in British North America, John's father moves his wife and four young children to Upper Canada when John is 5 years old.

The Macdonalds admire Quebec City's harbour from its famous fortress, the Citadel. After a brief stopover here (the capital of Lower Canada), the family and their belongings will be pulled on a barge all the way to Kingston in Upper Canada.

From rags to riches... to rags again

John Alexander Macdonald was born on January 11, 1815, in Glasgow, Scotland. His father, Hugh Macdonald, had grown up in a small town north of Inverness in Scotland, then moved to Glasgow (the biggest city in Scotland) hoping to find opportunities to make his fortune. He did find love and the opportunity to make a family, for he met and married Helen Shaw. Together, they had five children in eight years. Sadly, their first boy died in infancy, making John the eldest son. John had an elder sister, Margaret, and a younger brother and sister, James and Louisa.

1811
John's brother William is born.

1813
William dies. Sister Margaret is born.

1815
John is born in Scotland, a country renowned for the haunting sound of its bagpipes (shown here).

1816
Brother James is born.

1818
Sister Louisa is born.

1820
The family leaves Scotland for Canada.

1822
Brother James dies.

1824
The family settles in Glenora.

1825
John is sent to boarding school.

1829
John leaves school at age 14.

A loving family

John's father was a friendly, easygoing man with lots of ideas about how to make money. Though he was born a shopkeeper's son, he was very ambitious and felt he was capable of doing much more than running a store. Yet each new business he tried simply did not work out. In 1819, he was running a firm that manufactured cottons but, once again, business was terrible. Faced with another failing endeavour, and with children and a wife to support, he knew he needed to do something bold.

About that time, Hugh heard from relatives that there were many opportunities for enterprising people like himself in the colonies of British North America. That sparked his imagination! In 1820, Hugh and Helen packed all their belongings and moved with their four young children to **Upper Canada**. John was 5 years old.

John's life in North America

At first the Macdonalds settled in Kingston, where there were many other people from Scotland. They opened a store, but Hugh was no more successful in Canada than he had been in Scotland, and this business failed. Two years after the Macdonalds moved to Canada, another family tragedy struck: James, John's little brother, died after being hit by a drunken servant. This left 7-year-old John the only boy in the family.

After the failure of the Kingston store, Hugh moved his family to Hay Bay, and then to the pretty town of Glenora where he bought a stone mill. This time things worked out for him, at least for a while. The milling business was good for the Macdonalds and they lived in Glenora for ten years.

As Hugh finally prospered, he was able to afford more good things for his family and what he wanted to give John most was a proper education. But Hugh wasn't satisfied with the school nearby, so he sent his bright young son away to boarding school. Although John didn't like leaving his family, he enjoyed school. He loved to read and learn. But unfortunately, in those days local schooling ended at age 14 and only wealthy families could afford to send their children to England, Montreal, Fredericton, or Halifax to continue their educations. John's family just didn't have the money. Like other boys from ordinary families, he began working at age 15. "I had no boyhood," John once said. "From the age of 15 I had to earn my own living."

What was school like in the 1800s?

Although the first Canadian schools were built in the 1600s by the French who settled Quebec, formal education did not become widespread until the 1800s. At that time, the primary concern of schools was to preserve language, culture and religion.

Very few children went to school, either because they lived too far away from one or because their parents didn't have enough money to send them. You had to pay to attend school, which was considered a privilege, not a right like it is today! Most education took place at home. Children were mainly taught the responsibilities they would have to perform as adults, such as housework, labour, farming, or a trade.

What did kids learn in school when John was growing up? The three "R's" (Reading, wRiting and aRithmetic), penmanship, **Bible** stories, grammar, science, history, and languages such as Latin or French (John studied both). Sometimes boys and girls learned different subjects, with girls studying more of the arts.

The youngest students used books called **primers** to learn reading, but they soon advanced to using the Bible as their main book.

For writing they used a feather pen, called a quill, that they dipped in an inkwell. Imagine having to lift your pen from the inkwell to your paper without dripping. Now can you guess why they also used something called **blotting paper**? Inkwells had another infamous purpose: when the teacher's back was turned, mischievous boys could dip girls' hair-braids in them!

Sometimes boys and girls were seated separately in the classroom. It was also common for students to be seated according to age or ability. If you have the chance to look at one of the larger old school buildings, you may notice the word "Girls" carved above one entrance and "Boys" carved above the other. In some schools girls and boys used separate doors right into the 1950s!

Photo: Sesquicentennial Museum and Archives, Toronto District School Board.

1838

John is becoming well known because of his talents as a successful lawyer. His reputation grows even more when he becomes involved with several celebrated law cases.

The legal eagle becomes a political powerhouse

John disliked leaving school, but he was determined to make the best of it. He met a respected lawyer named George Mackenzie, who was so impressed with John's intelligence and drive that he hired John as an **apprentice**. This job would train John to become a lawyer himself. John did fantastic work and Mackenzie's law practice in Kingston prospered. When Mackenzie opened another office in Napanee, he chose his skillful 17-year-old apprentice to run it.

After a time, John left this job to take over the office of an ill cousin. John had kept his eyes open working for Mackenzie and continued to learn more while working in his cousin's office. In those days, you did not have to go to university to become a lawyer; you just had to pass the **bar examination**. With what he had learned from his jobs, John was able to pass the bar easily, and he soon opened a law office of his own in Kingston.

John became very well known in both Kingston and Napanee because of his talents as a lawyer. His reputation grew even more when he became involved in several celebrated law cases. One of them involved a number of Americans.

In 1838, approximately 600 rebels (including a few hundred Americans) tried to take control of Upper Canada. They were led by a Canadian, **William Lyon Mackenzie** (no relation to George Mackenzie, John's former employer). John actually took up arms to defend Canada against them! But he never fired a single shot. And you'll never guess what he did next: he turned around and defended many of these same raiders in court! Their trials were famous and soon so was John. It was a very smart move for his career and he shone in court. Despite losing many of these

1830
John becomes apprentice to George Mackenzie in Kingston.

1834
John opens his own law office.

1836
John takes the bar exam and becomes a qualified lawyer.

1843
John enters politics.

1856
John becomes joint Premier of the new Province of Canada.

1865
John drafts the British North America Act (Canadian Constitution) Its cover is shown here:

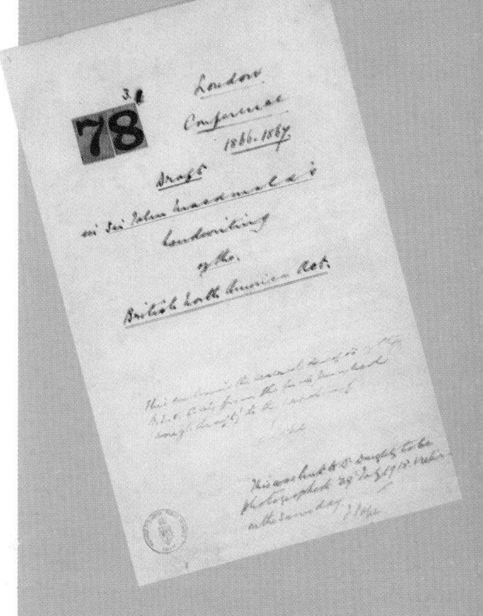

1867
The Dominion of Canada is created, and John becomes Sir John A. Macdonald and the first Prime Minister of Canada.

John loved to tell jokes, especially lawyer jokes.

Here's one of his favourites:

Why is tampering with sugar a worse crime than killing someone?

Murder is a gross offence, but tampering with sugar is a grocer offence!

cases – at a time when being convicted sometimes led to hanging – John's brilliant legal skills were praised to the skies. In one case, the court rewarded John's outstanding work by ordering a personal scaffold to be built for the condemned man! Soon everyone in Upper Canada knew who John was.

What makes a good leader?

In 1843, at the age of 28, John was elected as an **alderman** in Kingston. The next year he won a **seat in Parliament**. He worked hard in the government, building a reputation as a smart man who was great at convincing people to go along with his ideas. This hard work paid off for John. In 1854, he was one of the men chosen to create a new **political party**, the **Conservative Party of Canada**. He helped make the first-ever party that both English and French Canadians were happy to join together.

John's personality, intelligence, and incredible ability to connect with people made him a natural leader. His public speeches were legendary, with audiences cheering and laughing all the way through. He spoke words that touched people's hearts: "Let us remember the time of depression, the time of sinking hearts, empty pockets, and empty larders." He spoke words that inspired people's hopes: "Let us be English or let us be French... and above all let us be Canadians." But best of all, he spoke words that made everyone, even his enemies, laugh: "There are times when I do things that are against my conscience, but if I do not make certain allowances for the weakness of human nature, my party would turn me out of power, and those who took my place would manage things worse than I." Not surprisingly, John was hugely popular both with the powerful men in his community and with the working people.

How our country was made

In the middle 1800s, North America was made up of the United States of America (USA) in the southern half of the continent, and a number of separate British colonies in the north, known as **British North America**. Even though the majority of people who came to this huge continent had come from England, there were some major differences among them.

The colonies in British North America had very little to do with one another. Most of the settlers lived in the eastern part of the continent, in the colonies of New Brunswick, Newfoundland, and Nova Scotia. They were mainly farmers, fishers, fur traders, or lumberjacks, and made their living by trading with Britain.

There were also the two inland colonies of Upper Canada and **Lower Canada**, which Britain had united into a single colony in 1841. The new, combined colony was called the Province of Canada. The people in

Not called the 'First Nations' for nothing!

When the Europeans arrived in North America, they found it was already inhabited by many different and distinct tribes or nations. Each group had its own culture that evolved out of its environment and the resources available to it. Tribes near the oceans concentrated on fishing, those in the forests hunted, some farmed, and others followed herds of animals as they migrated.

The First Nations people were all very different but did share some common characteristics. One of these was the way their history was passed down from generation to generation by story-telling. Elders (wise healers and keepers of the tribe's traditions) were highly respected in their societies. Children learned, not by going to school, but by watching and helping the adults. Most native cultures also placed a higher value on the well-being of the group over the individual. That meant sharing and co-operating were more important than accumulating personal wealth. Someone was considered "wealthy" if he or she had good health, good friends and a place of honour.

In European societies, things were very different. Acquiring wealth and power was the goal. As soon as their explorers began to land in North America, they started to lay claim to native lands and resources and the future of native peoples began to change forever.

The philosophies of the European and the First Nations were very far apart. As Peau de Chat, a native chief explained "it was the Great Spirit who gave [the land] to us, from the time my ancestors came upon earth it has been considered ours." European nations disagreed and felt that native land was there for the taking.

The Canadian government negotiated with the First Nations peoples to buy their land. What seemed like a good idea at the time became a nightmare for many. The terms of the treaties made back in Sir John's time are still not settled today!

The words of George Erasmus, the Assembly of First Nations chief from 1985 to 1991, are truly inspiring: "We have the ability to create a country that will be envied...We have the ability to create a culture that will be different from others because we will take from each other and we will give to each other, but we will not have to crush each other."

For more information on Canada's First Nations peoples, visit www.jackfruitpress.com

1864

Might Canada actually become a country? Always open to discussion, the fathers of Confederation get together in Quebec City to work out a viable solution.

Canada West (formerly Upper Canada) spoke English, and those in Canada East (formerly Lower Canada) spoke French. Britain had hoped that unifying the two colonies would put an end to the use of the French language in North America. This didn't work, however, and the French settlers continued to speak their language and observe their traditions in the new province.

At the far west of the continent, separated from the other colonies by a vast expanse of land, British Columbia was more sparsely populated than the east.

The USA was formed from a union of former British colonies that had gone to war with Britain (the **American War of Independence**, 1775-1783) to break free from Britain and rule themselves. Most of the people in British North America preferred to remain part of the **British Empire** and they worried the USA would try to force the weaker colonies in British North America to join their union. They were also concerned that, even without force, the weaker colonies could be persuaded to join the larger, stronger USA.

For these reasons, a number of people started to talk about **Confederation** – making the many colonies in British North America into one unified country. They felt that forming their own strong nation made up of the colonies that wanted to remain aligned with Britain was the only way to continue to be part of the British Empire. At first John disagreed, but after consideration, he became one of Confederation's biggest supporters.

John pulls it all together

John worked hard to convince the leaders of the separate colonies they would be much better off together. By July 1866, most of the colonies had agreed. But Prince Edward Island and Newfoundland refused to join because they were afraid of losing their ability to govern themselves. On March 29, 1867, **Queen Victoria** signed the British North America Act. This Act created the Dominion of Canada on July 1, 1867, an event Canadians celebrate every July 1. The Queen also **knighted** John and asked him to form the first government of the new country.

1863
As Sir John's personal problems become worse, he turns to drinking. Unfortunately, his every move is reported in The Globe, Canada's most prominent newspaper.
"It's not drink that makes me sick but the rantings of my honourable opponent!"
Sir John throws up in the House of Commons. Using his characteristic wit, he surprises everyone by immediately claiming that his opponent's poor argument is what made his stomach turn! (Some sources say this incident happened elsewhere and on a different date.)

Troubles and triumphs in John's personal life

Love and marriage...

While John was working so hard at his career and public life, he also experienced challenges and victories in his personal life. His father had died in 1841, so in 1842 John went to Scotland to clear up some legal matters and visit the place where he was born. While travelling throughout Britain, he met his cousin **Isabella Clark**. They fell in love, and were married in Canada in 1843. John bought a house in Kingston, where the couple lived with John's mother and his sisters, Margaret and Louisa.

Within a year of moving to Canada, Isabella became ill. She was i n constant pain. In hope of finding a cure, John took her to stay with family in the warmer and drier climate of the state of Georgia in the USA. Happily, her health improved there.

...and family

Isabella and John stayed in the USA together for several months before John was forced to return to Canada because of work, leaving Isabella behind to recover. John visited her whenever he could get away from his law

1843
John marries Isabella Clark.

1844
Isabella becomes ill.

1847
Isabella and John have a baby boy, John Jr., in August.

1848
John Jr. dies.

1850
A second son, Hugh John, is born in March.

1857
Isabella Clark Macdonald dies, three days after Christmas.

ISABELLA CLARK
WIFE OF
JOHN A. MACDONALD
DIED DEC. 28, 1857
AGE 48 YRS.

1867
Sir John marries Susan Agnes Bernard.

1869
Sir John and Susan have a baby girl, Mary, in February.

1869
Sir John realizes that his business partner left him heavily in debt.

1870
Mary is discovered to have a severe disability.

practice and Parliament. In 1847, Isabella gave birth to a robust baby boy, John Jr. Although they were very happy when John Jr. arrived, the strain of the pregnancy had weakened Isabella. Her sister, **Maria Macpherson**, brought baby John home to Kingston to take care of him, because Isabella was too sick to travel. Although she was well enough to return home the next summer, in 1848, her health quickly declined until she was unable to leave her bed. Having to continue all his political duties without her at his side was lonely for John, especially at the many dinner parties and social events he was expected to attend.

As Isabella's health continued to deteriorate, suddenly more heartbreak hit the family: John Jr. died when he was only 13 months old. Despite grief for his son and growing worry about his wife, John stayed true to his nature and persevered, working hard to further his political career.

Two years later, Isabella and John had another child, **Hugh John Macdonald**. Thankfully, this child survived and lived a very long life.

As if his family problems weren't bad enough, like his father, John had constant money troubles. There just never seemed to be enough of it to manage. Here was the big dilemma: not only did the work of building a political career produce no income, but it left John little time to devote to his law practice. It didn't help that he'd spent a great deal of time in the USA trying to find doctors who could cure Isabella. Though at first he had a business partner who was happy to be with such a famous lawyer, in time the partner grew dissatisfied. John was not bringing much income into the business, yet he was taking out most of the money it generated! Eventually, John's partner left to form his own law practice.

Seeking false happiness in a bottle

Being the leader of a political party is, of course, very difficult. Add to it the daily stress of money problems and his wife's illness. John was longing for something to relieve his pressures, and he started to drink too much. While at first getting drunk may make the drinker feel like problems are going away, it's actually creating whole new, bigger problems of its own.

Isabella died in 1857, leaving John alone with 7-year-old Hugh. To numb his pain and escape the pressures of his life, John continued turning to alcohol, which kept making everything worse. His drinking problem became famous. When drunk, he did many embarrassing things in public, and these were always prominently reported in Toronto's most important newspaper, the *Globe*.

So in 1844, this guy called George Brown started a newspaper called The Globe.

And, like over 150 years later, people across Canada are still reading this paper. Except now it's called The Globe and Mail.

The Disease of Alcoholism

Alcoholism, or alcohol dependency, can be confusing. Alcohol is legal, but it is also classified as a drug (which means a person can become addicted to it). Many people are able to drink alcohol occasionally without it causing problems, but others cannot drink at all without losing control. Alcoholism is characterized by five signs (called symptoms):

1. A strong urge to drink alcohol (craving)
2. Not being able to stop drinking once the person has started (loss of control)
3. The need to drink more and more alcohol to get the same "high" (tolerance)
4. A bodily reaction when the person stops drinking: shaking, sweating, becoming nauseous, or anxious (withdrawal)
5. Problems with work, money, relationships, breaking the law, or dangerous behaviour such as violence or drunk driving

Why is it called a disease? Because, just like other diseases, it is chronic (lasts a person's lifetime), has the same symptoms in everyone, and follows a predictable path of development. It's also classified as a disease because the craving to drink that alcoholics feel can be as strong as the need for food or water. Stress, lifestyle, and genetics (other alcoholics in the family) are factors known to contribute to the problem. For example, Sir John had a lot of stress, and heavy drinking was a common part of the lifestyle of politicians in his day.

Is it serious? Alcoholism can destroy relationships and cause physical illness, including liver damage and death. Drinking during pregnancy can cause severe **birth defects** to the fetus. Drinking and driving can cause car accidents, sometimes fatal ones.

Unfortunately, in Sir John's time, alcoholism was poorly understood and looked upon as a character flaw. No effective treatment was available. Some people (called teetotallers) thought all alcohol should be banned and formed **temperance societies** to make drinking illegal.

Can alcoholism be helped now? You bet it can! Doctors help with counselling and medications that control the alcohol cravings. Alcoholics Anonymous (AA) is an organization that provides an awesomely successful twelve-step program, for free, in 150 countries worldwide. AA was founded in 1935 by a stockbroker and a surgeon who both recovered from alcoholism, and then wanted to help others turn their lives around, too. Inspiring!

For more information about alcohol dependency, including numbers you can phone for help with alcohol concerns, please visit our website at www.jackfruitpress.com

The paper was run by **George Brown**, one of John's most famous and vocal enemies. Hoping to destroy John's political career, Brown wrote tirades such as this: "Macdonald is mentally unwell; he tried to commit suicide at Rivière du Loup; he has few lucid moments." The next day, Sir John began a speech with his trademark wit and honesty: "Ladies and gentlemen, in one of my lucid moments, I now address you." No matter how badly he behaved or how often Brown wrote about him, John continued to prosper in politics.

Love again – and more family

In February of 1867, when John was 52, he married **Susan Agnes Bernard**. She was a healthy, lively woman who was 30 years old. Two years later they had a child named **Margaret Mary Theodora Macdonald**, whom everyone called Mary. She was the delight of her father's life, but before long it was discovered she had been born with hydrocephalus (often called "water on the brain" back then) and that she would need a wheelchair to get around. There was a great deal of prejudice against people with disabilities in those days. Some people ridiculed John for adoring Mary and spending so much time with her. He nicknamed her "Baboo" and read to her before dinner each afternoon. He brought her into the House of Commons to hear him speak. And he agonized over how hard she had to work to achieve the usual childhood developments most people can take for granted. Father and daughter were close for the rest of his life, writing each other affectionate letters when they were apart. Contrary to doctors' expectations – and no doubt due to the love and support of her family – Mary lived to age 65.

Ottawa, August 25, 1873

My dearest Mary,

You must know that your kind Mamma and I are very anxious to see you and Granny again. We have put a new carpet in your room and got everything ready for you.

There are some fine melons in the garden. You must pick them for dinner and feed the chickens with the rind. You remember that Mamma cut my hair and made me look like a cropped donkey. It has grown quite long again. When you come home, you must not pull it too hard.

Give my love to dear good Grand Mamma and give her a kiss for me. Give my love to Sarah too, and so good bye my pet and come home soon to

your loving Papa

As if he hadn't faced enough challenges, once again, Sir John had trouble with a law partner. A.J. MacDonell, John's partner of many years, died leaving many bills unpaid. At the age of 54, just when John thought his money problems were over, he was shocked to discover the business owed $80,000! In today's money, that would be like owing $1 million. John had to repay it all. This might have stopped a lesser man, but it did not stop John.

The murder of Thomas D'Arcy McGee is one of the most shocking moments in Sir John's life.

1868

Rushing to the scene of the murder, on Sparks Street in Ottawa, Sir John holds his dear friend's dead body. An unknown assassin has just shot D'Arcy as he was returning home from a late-night session of Parliament.

1867

As the population of the USA keeps growing, many Americans begin to feel it is their right to expand and occupy the entire continent of North America.

A small group of Irish-American Fenians sneak across the border to raid a Canadian settlement.

The new dominion is threatened

Only two years before the colonies of British North America were made into a country, a **civil war** had finished between the northern and southern states of the USA. But after the northern states won, many Americans felt it was their right to expand and occupy the entire continent of North America. This thinking was called **manifest destiny**.

Since Britain had not supported the North during the Civil War, American newspapers based in the victorious North angrily urged their leaders to take military revenge on Britain by attacking its colonies. All of this was going on while Sir John was trying to unite the colonies into a confederation.

Trouble from America

The Americans weren't just making threats in their newspapers. Small groups of Irish-Americans were coming across the border trying to carry out those threats! These attacks were called the **Fenian raids**, and Sir John thought that the American government didn't do enough to prevent them. These raids started in 1866, the year before Queen Victoria created the **Dominion of Canada**. Fenians invaded two more times, in 1870 and 1871. Each time, they were defeated or they withdrew before Canadian forces arrived.

At first, the Dominion of Canada was made up of four provinces: Ontario, New Brunswick, Nova Scotia, and Quebec. Their combined population was 4 million. Intense talks were still going on about how to get the other colonies to join the new country.

In the midst of all this, the Americans were negotiating with Russia to purchase a territory called Alaska. In 1867, they closed the deal. But what

1866-71
Irish-Americans raid Canada to overthrow British rule in Ireland.

1869
Canada purchases Rupert's Land for $1.5 million.

1870
Louis Riel leads the Red River Rebellion. Riel's deerskin jacket is show here.

Manitoba and the Northwest Territories are created from Rupert's Land.

1871
British Columbia joins Canada.

1873
Prince Edward Island joins Canada.

1873
Pacific Scandal: Sir John resigns in disgrace.

1873-78
New Prime Minister Mackenzie decides to stop the railway project.

1870

about the great expanse of land in between the northwest USA and Alaska? At the time, it was called Rupert's Land and was controlled by the Hudson's Bay Company. Naturally, the USA wanted this territory to connect its northwest lands with the newly purchased Alaska. But both Britain and Sir John were determined this vast region should become part of Canada instead.

The Americans had offered $30 million for Rupert's Land, but Canada came up with a better offer. Canada paid the company $1.5 million in cash and allowed them to keep ownership of large portions of the land, which they were free to develop and sell later to individuals or companies. It was a good way for Canada to get the land and for the company to make money.

The Métis (and other settlers in Manitoba and the Northwest Territories) fear the new railway will bring in settlers who will take their lands. They ask the Macdonald government for help. When a response is slow in coming, Louis Riel leads the Métis to rebel against Canadian rule.

But this purchase didn't settle all the problems. Most of the people living on that land did not want to be part of Canada or the USA! They wanted things to stay exactly as they were.

Trouble in Canada

Most of the people who lived on what had been Rupert's Land were Métis: settlers and fur trappers who were half European (mostly French-Canadian) and half First Nations people. They wanted to continue to live the way they always had and were worried that if they became part of Canada, the English people would take away their land. In fact, representatives from Canada did come to survey (get information about) the land and to record who owned it. The Métis had their own system for land ownership, but the surveyors ignored it and were very disrespectful to boot. This made the Métis even more afraid they were in danger of losing the land they had lived on for generations.

The Hudson's Bay Company started in 1670 and it's still one of the biggest companies in Canada.

The Métis asked **Louis Riel** to be their leader. Riel set up a **provisional government** to represent the Métis. When Sir John sent William McDougall to survey about the new territory, Louis Riel told him to leave because the Métis had not agreed to be ruled by Canada. He said they had their own government and did not need any interference from Ottawa.

Not everyone was sympathetic to the Métis. Some people who lived in the Red River area of this territory did want to be part of Canada. One of these people was **Thomas Scott**. He caused a riot and was put in jail. While he was in jail, he caused even more trouble, and Riel's provisional government ordered him to be executed by firing squad.

When the people in the rest of English-speaking Canada heard about Scott's execution, they demanded that Riel be hanged as a traitor. But the French-speaking people of Quebec disagreed. They thought Riel had the right to rule and to deal with prisoners in his own way since he was leader of the provisional government.

Sir John decided it was best to negotiate with the Métis rather than wage a war. He did not treat Riel like a traitor, and instead, agreed to leave most of the land to the Métis and the First Nations peoples. He formed the Northwest Territories out of most of the land, and created Manitoba from a small portion in the south.

Caught with his hand in the cookie jar

Meanwhile, the government of British Columbia wanted a road to connect that colony to the existing provinces of Canada so that commerce and communication would be easier and more practical. The BC government wanted the road building to start within three years. But when its representatives went to the government of Canada to discuss the terms for BC to join, they asked for a railway instead of a roadway. The Canadian government agreed to this, and even promised to start it within two years rather than three. This made the British Columbians very happy and they agreed to join Canada in 1871.

Many companies wanted the very profitable contract to build the railway. But none wanted it more than **Hugh Allan's Canadian Pacific Railway Company**. As the government was deciding whom to award the contract

Mifflin Wistar Gibbs was part of the delegation that decided BC should join Canada instead of the USA.

Since Mifflin was black, that says a lot about his determination to overcome racial prejudice...

...at a time when African-Americans were just barely coming out of slavery.

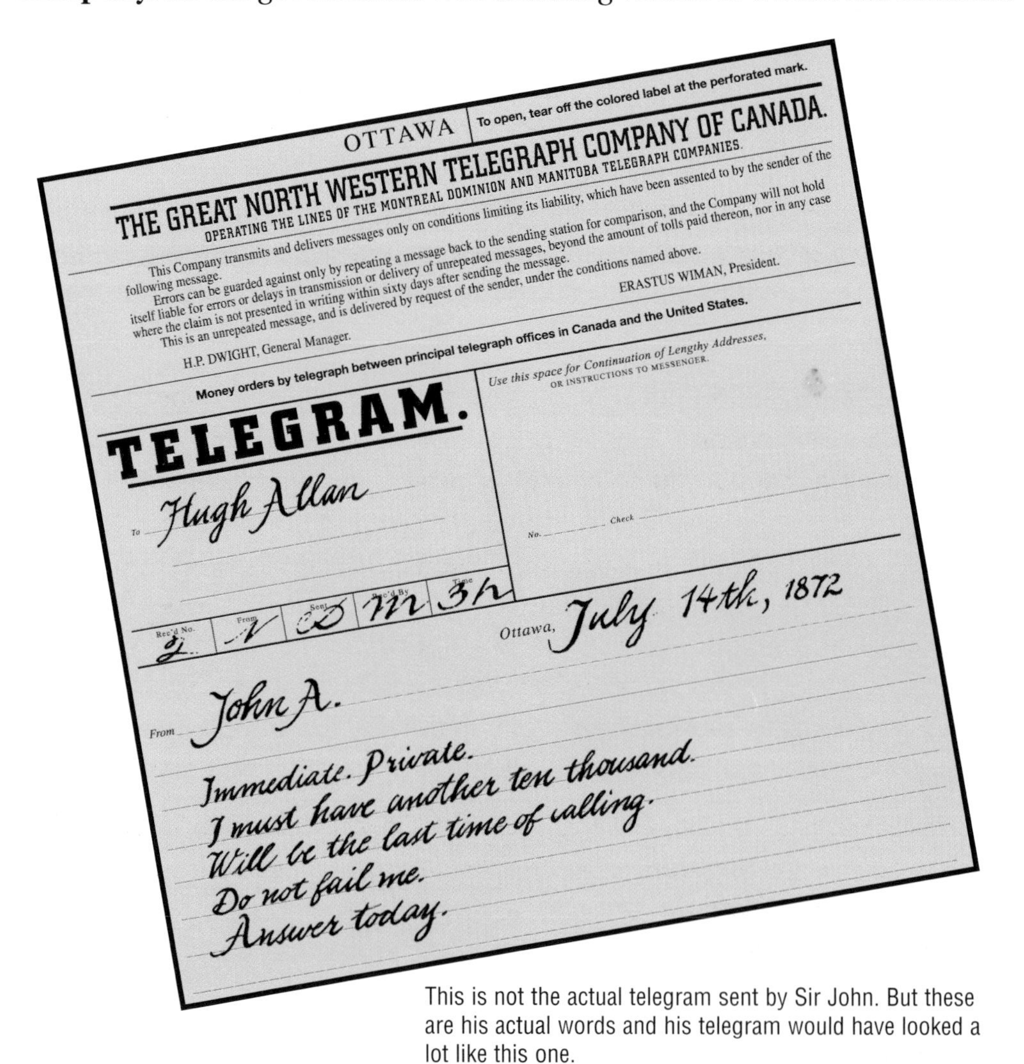
OTTAWA | To open, tear off the colored label at the perforated mark.

THE GREAT NORTH WESTERN TELEGRAPH COMPANY OF CANADA.
OPERATING THE LINES OF THE MONTREAL DOMINION AND MANITOBA TELEGRAPH COMPANIES.

This Company transmits and delivers messages only on conditions limiting its liability, which have been assented to by the sender of the following message.
Errors can be guarded against only by repeating a message back to the sending station for comparison, and the Company will not hold itself liable for errors or delays in transmission or delivery of unrepeated messages, beyond the amount of tolls paid thereon, nor in any case where the claim is not presented in writing within sixty days after sending the message.
This is an unrepeated message, and is delivered by request of the sender, under the conditions named above.

H.P. DWIGHT, General Manager. ERASTUS WIMAN, President.

Money orders by telegraph between principal telegraph offices in Canada and the United States.

Use this space for Continuation of Lengthy Addresses, OR INSTRUCTIONS TO MESSENGER.

TELEGRAM.

To Hugh Allan

Ottawa, July 14th, 1872

From John A.

Immediate. Private.
I must have another ten thousand.
Will be the last time of calling.
Do not fail me.
Answer today.

This is not the actual telegram sent by Sir John. But these are his actual words and his telegram would have looked a lot like this one.

to, it was also planning for an election. As is true today, elections cost a lot of money. The political parties had to print signs and placards, rent meeting halls, and pay for the many other expenses of convincing people to vote for their candidates.

In those days, people did not vote using a written secret **ballot** as we do today. Instead, they would attend an election meeting and shout out the name of the candidate they wanted. In order to make sure he won the next election, Macdonald and the Conservative party decided to pay people to vote for him. To do this, they needed money.

Knowing it would make the Conservative party grateful to him, Hugh Allan gave the party around $300,000 for the election campaign. That would be the same as giving $5 million today. Surprisingly, even this huge amount was not enough for Sir John! He sent a telegram to Allan demanding, "I must have another ten thousand. Will be the last time of calling. Do not fail me. Answer me today."

Two men broke into the office of Allan's lawyer, stole the telegram, and sold it to the opposing **Liberal Party of Canada** for $5,000 cash. They also told the press about the message in the telegram. Soon headlines in newspapers across the country proclaimed that the Conservative party had received very large sums of money from a company that had gotten a very profitable contract from the government. Giving a contract to a company that had donated a lot of money to your political party was (and is still) considered unethical and improper. The publicity created quite a scandal (they called it the **Pacific Scandal**) and Sir John was smack in the middle of it.

Disgrace!

Sir John A. Macdonald's political life was ruined! He was so upset that he disappeared and no one, not even his wife, knew where he was. Many people thought he was so ashamed that he had killed himself. But he showed up ten days later and admitted his party had taken the money. He tried to convince people that the money was not the reason he gave Allan's company the contract to build the national railway, but Canadians did not believe him. With the country angry over the scandal, Macdonald and his government resigned in disgrace on November 5, 1873. Many people thought this would be the end of both the railway and Sir John's career in politics.

The **Governor General** asked the Liberal leader, **Alexander Mackenzie**, to form a new government. Alexander Mackenzie became the second Prime Minister of Canada. But this was not the last Canada would hear of Sir John A. Macdonald.

So what do you think would happen today if someone found out a company gave a political party over $5 million and, say, they just happened to get a big, fat contract in return?

Think they should make a law against that?

Surprise, they did! Starting on January 1, 2004, corporations could only donate $1,000 a year. Individuals can only donate $5,000 a year.

1873

Sir John has caused a scandal by accepting bribes (illegal sums of money) for granting railroad-building contracts. Because of this, he thinks his party should choose another leader.

Sir John shows up at the offices of the Ottawa Citizen to announce his resignation. The newspaper's editor refuses to publish his decision.

Down, but not out

Sir John wanted the best for his party and thought his Conservative followers should choose another leader because of the scandal he had caused. But his followers would hear none of this and refused to let him resign! They still believed wholeheartedly that he was the best person to run their party and the government of Canada. By 1878, the Liberals had introduced many new laws to make the government more honest. But the party had become unpopular because economic times were hard. So Alexander Mackenzie's government called an election – which Sir John saw as the perfect opportunity to regain his position as Prime Minister.

A brilliant plan

Sir John proposed a **National Policy** that would put a tax on American goods. This would make them more expensive than the same kinds of Canadian goods. Sir John said this tax would help Canadian farmers, factories, and workers because people would buy Canadian-made products instead of American ones.

The Liberals disagreed with this plan, but the idea made sense to the people of Canada. When the election was over, Mackenzie was very surprised to find that he had lost and the Conservative party, with Sir John at the reins, was returned to power.

More good work, more trouble

Once again head of the country, Sir John resumed the railway project. It was finally completed at 9:22 a.m. on November 7, 1885. Now settlers and goods could easily reach western Canada. The railway had become an important symbol for the unity of Canada from coast to coast.

Though most Canadians were very happy with the new railway, from the point of view of the Métis and other settlers in what is now Saskatchewan and the Northwest Territories, it was a terrible threat, bringing in settlers who wanted to take their land. They knew the Canadian government might not recognize their claims to the land because their methods of

1873-78
Sir John A. Macdonald continues to lead the Conservative party.

1878
The Conservatives win the election. Sir John is Prime Minister of Canada once again.

1885
Canada's first national park is created in Banff.

1885
Canada's national railway is completed.

1885
Louis Riel leads the unsuccessful Northwest Rebellion.

1886
Riel is hanged as a traitor.

1891
On June 6, Sir John dies at the age of 76.

November 7, 1885: Driving the last spike to complete the Canadian Pacific Railway.

dividing it and recording ownership were different. So the Métis and First Nations peoples petitioned the government of Canada for help. When a response was slow in coming, they grew impatient. And worried. And then they asked Louis Riel to help them once again. Riel agreed, and for two months his men rebelled against Canadian rule.

A questionable decision

This time Riel was not successful. Sir John had set up a police force in the area and was able to use the railway to send extra troops to fight against Riel and his rebel force. Riel was captured and charged with treason.

Many Canadians, who had not forgiven Riel for ordering the execution of Thomas Scott, thought Riel should be hanged as a traitor. Others, particularly the Métis and the people of Quebec, saw him as a hero. Riel's lawyers wanted him to plead insanity because he suffered from **mental illness** at the time. Feeling this would be disgraceful, Riel refused.

The jury at his trial found Riel guilty but recommended that he be treated with mercy. Sir John disagreed. In 1886, Riel and eight other First Nations leaders from the rebellion were hanged. Other leaders **Poundmaker** and **Big Bear** were imprisoned. Their spirits broken, they quickly contracted diseases in jail and died shortly after release. Many people still think Sir John was wrong to allow Riel to be executed. They

Chinese workers and the building of the CPR

From 1800 through1885, the hard labour of thousands of Chinese workers helped build the Canadian Pacific Railway. Shamefully, they were paid less than half the wage white men earned. Tragically, they were assigned the most dangerous tasks: tunnelling and handling explosives. More than 1,000 brave Chinese men died on the job.

But the rich history of Chinese Canadians dates back farther, to the year 1788. The first Chinese peoples to settle in Canada travelled with sea captain John Meares. They helped establish a trading post for otter pelts between Canton, China, and Nootka Sound, British Columbia.

During the 1800s, many people in China were having problems getting land, which meant they couldn't grow enough food to feed their families. Faced with such dire poverty at home, when their villages were visited by agents recruiting labourers for the CPR, many rushed at the chance to build a better life for their families. Trusting the agents' promises of good wages and permanent settlement, approximately 5,000 men signed on to move to Canada and build the railroad. Around 7,000 more came from California.

Once here, they quickly earned the reputation of being very hard workers. They sent money back to help their families in China, and saved to bring them to Canada as soon as possible. But reuniting with their loved ones became much more difficult in 1885, when the government passed the Chinese Immigration Act. Nicknamed the "Chinese Head Tax," it forced all Chinese immigrants to pay money to enter Canada. Despite the tax being very unpopular, the government didn't change it until 1947, more than sixty years later! To fight for equality, the Chinese formed organizations such as the **Chinese Consolidated Benevolent Association**. Canadians of **Asian** origin were not allowed to vote until 1948.

Amazing Chinese-Canadian Facts:

- Early Chinese immigrants called Canada "Gam San" (the Gold Mountain), because of the opportunity to advance themselves through hard work here.
- Canada's oldest Chinatown is in Victoria, British Columbia, and dates to 1858. Today it is the second largest Chinatown outside of Asia!
- Many of the medicines we use today are forms of herbal remedies that the Chinese have used for thousands of years!

For more information about Chinese-Canadian history, please visit our website at www.jackfruitpress.com

1885

Sir John is very successful at talking to extremely large crowds. He can project his voice to make himself heard by everyone. He also fills his speeches with amusing stories, passionate pleas, and exciting ideas.

An astute campaigner, Sir John uses a train station as a stage for yet another speech to a massive gathering in which he highlights the importance of having a national railroad.

think he should have dealt more favourably with the Métis land claims and negotiated a second settlement with Riel. Sir John did what he believed was best for Canada, but in a country with different kinds of people and different points of view, it can be hard to agree on what decision is right or wrong. What do you think Sir John should have done?

What do you think would have happened if Canada had become part of the great big US of A?

A final triumph

In 1891, Sir John called an election. During the campaign, he accused the Liberals of being traitors. He claimed that they were secretly meeting with the president of the USA. He produced posters making this claim and found a pamphlet to use as evidence against the Liberal party. The pamphlet was written by Edward Farrar, a Liberal who had indeed visited the American president. Farrar had written a report on the trip and presented the situation in a way that was favourable to the American point of view. Sir John declared that the Liberals were trying to sell Canada to the Americans.

Other Conservative posters were designed to show Sir John as being a loyal Canadian. He also made a famous speech to show how proud he was of his British and Canadian roots:

> *As for myself, my course is clear: A* ***British subject*** *I was born – a British subject I will die. With my utmost effort, with my latest breath, will I oppose "veiled treason" which attempts by sordid means and mercenary proffers to lure people from their allegiance…*

Sir John won the election of March 5, 1891, with this campaign, but during it he became very ill. By April 29, he had recovered enough to escort his son, Hugh John Macdonald, into the House of Commons as a new MP. But a month later, at 76 years of age, Sir John suffered a stroke and died on Saturday, June 6, 1891. Thousands of Canadians lined the railroad tracks to pay their respects to his funeral train. He was buried next to his mother in Cataraqui Cemetery, near Kingston, Ontario.

Exciting times in the making of

Canada was (and remains) an unusual country. Unlike many other, older countries, Canada was not created by people of one single race or culture. Best of all, no one single group persisted in forcing the others to become like them. Early in their history, Canadians learned that cooperation and mutual respect would work better than intolerance and confrontation.

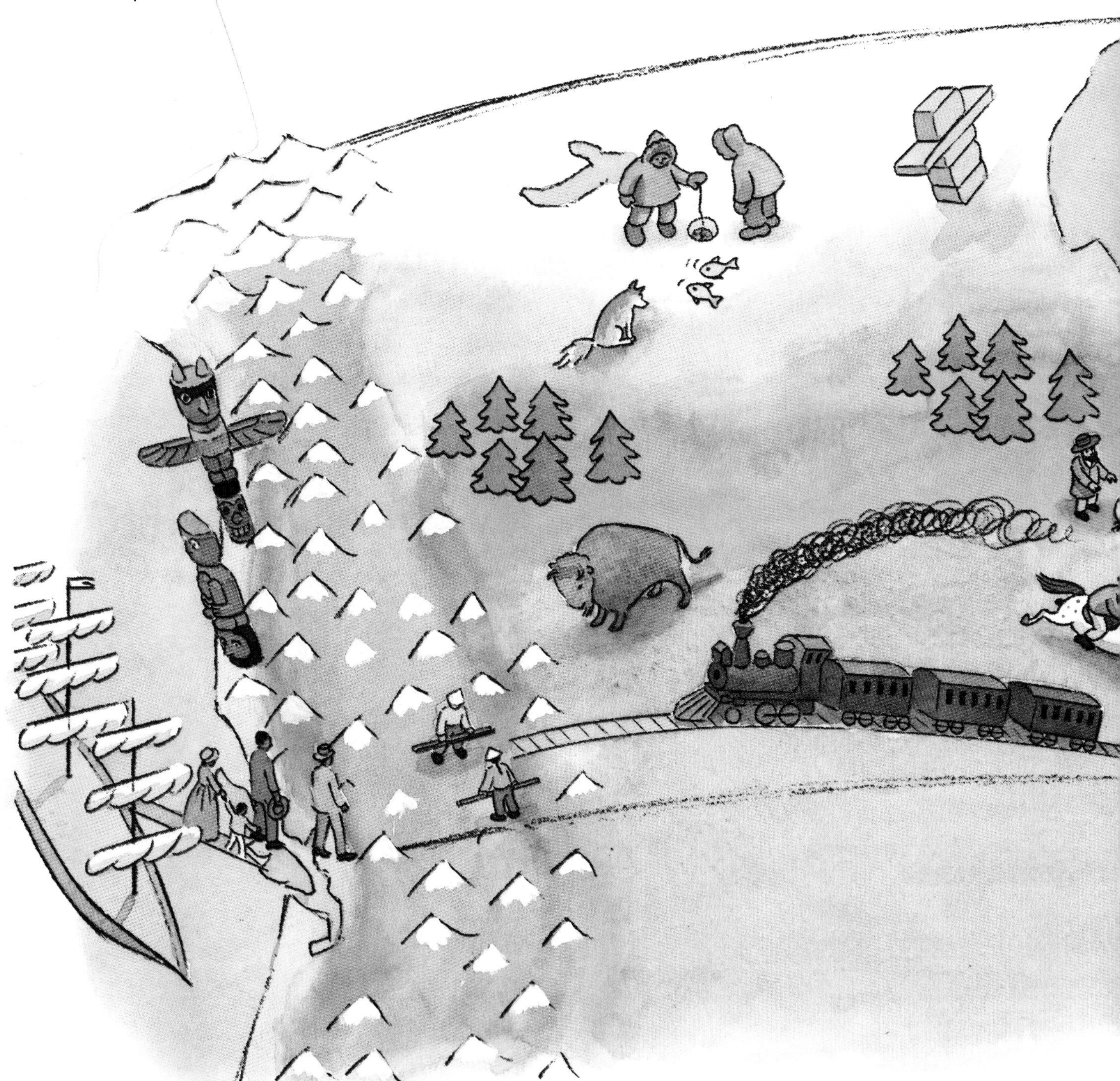

Check out some of the many events going on all over Canada during Sir John's life:

1. Fathers of Confederation meet in Charlottetown
2. Polishing the Constitution in Québec City
3. Squabbling over the border in New Brunswick
4. Erecting the Parliament buildings in Ottaw
5 Fenians raid a settlement near Kingston
6. American slaves flee to freedom

great country.

Things have been this way almost from the very beginning. For instance, Canada's various provinces had to be talked into joining as one country. And it took an extra 82 years before Newfoundland joined Confederation. This map shows this uniquely Canadian diversity at work during Sir John's life.

7. Red River Métis rebel against Ottawa
8. Chinese workers build a railway across the West
9. 800 African-Americans arrive in Victoria

Do you know where these events took place? To check your answers consult www.jackfruitpress.com

Sir John: the man who dreame

Sir John A. Macdonald was one of the most important people involved in building the Dominion of Canada. His skills of organizing and getting people to cooperate helped make peace between the French and the English. He brought Ontario, Quebec, New Brunswick, Nova Scotia, Prince Edward Island, British Columbia, the Northwest Territories, Manitoba, Alberta, Saskatchewan, and the Yukon into the union. Only Newfoundland joined Confederation without his involvement.

Many future leaders studied how Sir John worked and admired his ability to make friends and get things done. They marveled at how he used humour to turn difficult situations to his advantage. His way of handling people and problems was so effective that they copied his style. Even his opponents, such as the Liberal party leader and future Prime Minister **Wilfrid Laurier,** admired his intelligence and leadership abilities.

Sir John was truly a Canadian hero. He left behind a strong nation that has continued to grow and prosper. Many historians say he was one of the greatest Prime Ministers this country has ever had. What do you think?

Maybe the next time you see Sir John's picture on a $10 bill or pass his statue in a park, you'll remember the story of this Canadian hero. Maybe you'll think about how he kept working his way forward to create a better country no matter how much difficulty faced him. Maybe you'll remember the power of a dream... and wonder where your own dreams are leading you.

nd schemed a country

"I can, at my age, have no other wish
than to live well in the minds
of my fellow-countrymen, and when I die
to live well in their recollection. [cheers]

I have had a long life of politics, a long life of
official duties. I have committed many mistakes.

Looking back with the light of experience,
there are many things I have done wrongly,
and many things I have neglected
that I should have done.

In every act of legislation and administration,
I have tried, according to the best of my judgement,
to do what I could for the well-being
of good government and the future prosperity
of this, my beloved country."

This is part of a speech Sir John made to the working people of Toronto on May 30, 1881.

Timeline: The life and times of John A. Macdonald

YEAR	JOHN'S LIFE	EVENTS IN CANADA AND THE WORLD
1815	John A. is born in Glasgow, Scotland, on January 10 or 11.	
1818		The 49th parallel becomes the border between British North America and the USA.
1820	The Macdonald family moves to Kingston, Upper Canada.	George IV is crowned King of England.
1821		The Hudson's Bay Company merges with the Northwest Company of Montreal. As a result, many Métis lose their jobs.
1822	John's brother, James, dies.	
1824		Construction of the Welland Canal begins.
1825	The Macdonald family settles in Glenora.	
1826		Construction of the Rideau Canal begins.
1829	John leaves school at age 14.	The Lachine Canal opens in Montreal. Construction of the first Welland Canal is completed.
1830	John starts to work as an apprentice to Kingston lawyer George Mackenzie.	July Revolution in Paris, France: people rebel in reaction to price hikes, wage cuts, unemployment, and the laws of King Charles X .
1831		A law establishing the first railway in Canada is passed. The railway runs from La Prairie to St. John's, Quebec.
1832	George Mackenzie puts 17-year-old John in charge of his new law office in Napanee.	
1833	George Mackenzie dies. John opens his own law office.	The *Royal William* becomes the first steamship to cross the Atlantic Ocean. Great Britain abolishes slavery in the British West Indies.
1834	John, aged 19, is called to the Bar of Upper Canada.	William Lyon Mackenzie is elected the first mayor of Toronto. Slavery officially ends in all British colonies on July 31.
1836		Canada's first railway line is officially opened.
1837		In England, Victoria is crowned Queen. Britain tries to unite the colonies of Upper and Lower Canada. In reaction, both Canadas rebel. William Lyon Mackenzie (leader of the Reformers) leads the Upper Canada rebellion. Louis-Joseph Papineau (leader of the Patriotes) leads the Lower Canada rebellion. Both rebellions fail.
1838	Lawyer John defends American raiders of the Rebellion of 1837.	The Battle of Blood River, South Africa: the Boers confiscate Zulu land and force many Zulus to work on plantations as slaves.
1839		Lord Durham's report to the British Parliament suggests the union of Upper and Lower Canada, the assimilation of the French majority in Lower Canada, and the creation of an independent government. The Aroostook War occurs: New Brunswick and the American state of Maine fight over their boundary. First Opium War starts. It lasts until 1842.

More on the life and times of John A. Macdonald

YEAR	JOHN'S LIFE	EVENTS IN CANADA AND THE WORLD
1841	John's father dies. John travels to England and Scotland to settle legal matters. He meets his cousin Isabella Clark while abroad.	The Queen sanctions the union of Upper and Lower Canada under a central government. Upper Canada's name is changed to Canada West. Lower Canada's name is changed to Canada East. The Dawn Settlement is established to provide refuge for former slaves from the USA.
1842	John's law practice is now one of the busiest in Canada.	The Northeastern Boundary Dispute between New Brunswick and Maine is settled by the Webster-Ashburton Treaty. Construction of the first railway in Nova Scotia begins.
1843	Aged 28, John becomes an alderman on the Kingston Town Council. He marries Isabella Clark.	Fort Victoria is built by Britain to strengthen its claim to Vancouver Island. The Cornwall and Chambly Canals are officially opened.
1844	John is elected as a Conservative representative to the Legislative Assembly of Canada West.	Construction of the first railway in New Brunswick begins.
1845		The second Welland Canal is officially opened.
1846		British Prime Minister Robert Peel announces Free Trade. This ends the old colonial trading system.
1847	John becomes the Receiver General for the Province of Canada in May (1847–1848). His son, John, is born.	The St. Lawrence Canal is completed.
1848	John's son, John, dies.	Responsible government is granted to the Province of Canada.
1850	John's second son, Hugh John Macdonald, is born.	The Fugitive Slave Act is passed in the USA. This results in more free and enslaved black people fleeing to British North America.
1854	John becomes Attorney General for Canada West (1854–1867).	Reciprocity begins between British North America and the USA. The Crimean War takes place in the Balkans and the Crimean Peninsula (1854–1856): Russia fights the Ottoman (Turkish) Empire and its allies (Britain, France and Sardinia). Many soldiers die needlessly due to terrible hospital conditions before Florence Nightingale introduces modern nursing methods.
1855	John moves to Toronto, the capital city of the Province of Canada.	Bytown is renamed Ottawa.
1856		The Second Opium War (1856–1860) takes place: China fights Britain and France in an attempt to end the opium trade.
1857	John serves as joint Premier (with George-Étienne Cartier) for the Province of Canada (1857–1862). John's first wife, Isabella Clark Macdonald, dies.	The revolt of 1857: India fights for freedom from British rule. The issues are exploitive colonial laws that keep Indians impoverished and British army violations of the religious customs of Hindu and Muslim soldiers.
1859		Abraham Shadd becomes the first black person elected to public office.

Still more on the life and times of John A. Macdonald

YEAR	JOHN'S LIFE	EVENTS IN CANADA AND THE WORLD
1860		Construction begins on the House of Commons. The Maori Wars (1860-1872) begin: The Maori of New Zealand fight to keep their land from British settlers. Large areas of land are confiscated, causing permanent damage to Maori society. The American Civil War (1860-1865): President Lincoln and the northern states want to abolish slavery. The southern states form a provisional "Confederate" government and go to war against the North. The North wins and slavery is ended. Several Fenian raids into Canada take place.
1861	John is Minister of Militia Affairs (until 1867).	
1862	John's mother, Helen Shaw Macdonald, dies.	
1864	John attends the Confederation Conference in Charlottetown. He serves as co-leader (with George-Étienne Cartier and George Brown) of the Great Coalition (1864–1867).	
1865	John drafts most of the British North America (BNA) Act.	
1866		Several Fenian raids take place on the border with the USA.
1867	 John is the Liberal-Conservative party leader (1867–1891) and becomes Prime Minister at age 57 (1867–1873). John marries Susan Agnes Bernard.	**John A. Macdonald becomes the first Prime Minster of Canada (1867–1873)**
1868	D'Arcy McGee is murdered.	The First Federal Militia Act creates the first Canadian Army.
1869	John's daughter, Mary, is born.	
1870		The Red River Rebellion takes place. Thomas Scott is executed under Louis Riel's Provisional Government. The Northwest Territories and the province of Manitoba are created.
1871	 John goes to Washington as a member of a British Commission.	British Columbia joins Confederation. Treaty Number 1 is signed on July 25. Treaty Number 2 is signed on August 17.
1872		The first nationwide labour protest is held. Asian and Native peoples are banned from voting in BC.

Even more on the life and times of John A. Macdonald

YEAR	JOHN'S LIFE	EVENTS IN CANADA AND THE WORLD
1873	John is forced to resign as Prime Minister because of the Pacific Scandal. He becomes leader of the Opposition (1873–1878).	The Northwest Mounted Police is formed. The Pacific Scandal takes place. Prince Edward Island joins Confederation. Alexander Mackenzie is elected the 2nd Prime Minister of Canada (November 7, 1873–October 8, 1878).
1875		The Supreme Court of Canada is established. The Indian Act is passed.
1876	John's sister Margaret dies.	
1877		Manzo Nagano is the first official Japanese immigrant to Canada. The Russian-Turkish War (1877–1878) takes place: a continuation of a series of wars between Russia and the Ottoman Empire over land boundaries.
1878	John is elected Prime Minister again (1878–1891). He also becomes Minister of the Interior (1878–1883) and serves as Superintendent General of Indian Affairs (1878–1887).	The Canada Temperance Act is passed. **John A. Macdonald is elected for a second term as Prime Minister of Canada (1878–1891).**
1879		The Anglo-Zulu War takes place in South Africa. Britain wins and takes over control of Zululand. The War of the Pacific (1879–1883): Peru, Bolivia and Chile fight over borders and natural resources.
1880		Emily Stowe becomes the first woman doctor to practise in Canada.
1883		The Sino French War starts (1883–1885): France and China fight over Vietnam. In the end, Vietnam is divided: China controls the South, France gets the North.
1885		The Canadian Pacific Railway is completed. Canada's first national park is created in Banff, Alberta. The Northwest Rebellion continues. Louis Riel is hanged for treason. The federal government imposes a tax on Chinese immigrants.
1888		The Fisheries Treaty is passed. The first elections take place in the Northwest Territories.
1890	John's younger sister, Louisa, dies.	The Manitoba School Act is passed.
1891	John wins the election of 1891. He dies on June 6 at age 76.	John Abbott becomes the third Prime Minister of Canada (1891–1892).

Glossary: words and facts you might want to know.

Allan, Sir Hugh (1810–1882): a very rich businessman who made large donations to influence the federal government to give him the contract to build a transcontinental railway. When news of this influence hit the press in 1873, it created the Pacific Scandal and forced John A. Macdonald's government to resign.

alcoholism: a disease that causes someone to have an extreme desire to drink alcohol, even when it causes physical, social, and emotional problems.

alderman: an elected member of a city council who is next in line to the mayor.

American War of Independence (1775–1781): a conflict in which the 13 American colonies (now states) revolted against their British rulers. In 1783, Great Britain signed a formal treaty recognizing their independence as the United States of America (USA).

Asian: relating to the continent of Asia or its people. Asia is the world's largest continent and includes the countries of China, India, Japan, and Korea, to name a few.

ballot: the piece of paper upon which a voter writes his/her vote.

bar examination: the test that people must pass in order to practise law. When law students successfully complete their university training, articling (apprenticeship in a law firm), and bar examination, they are "called to the bar," that is, allowed to join the professional bar association of their province. This authorizes them to practise law.

Bernard, Susan Agnes (1836–1920): second wife of Sir John A. Macdonald. They married in 1867 and had one daughter, Margaret Mary Theodora. Susan moved with Mary to England after John's death. She died in England and was buried in Eastbourne, a city just south of London.

Bible: the sacred scriptures and teachings of Christians comprising the Old Testament and the New Testament.

Big Bear (1825–1888): Odjibwe/Cree leader of First Nations people in what is now called Saskatchewan. He advocated for gathering Plains Native peoples together onto a massive reserve instead of small, scattered ones as the Canadian government proposed. He only signed a treaty in 1876 to sell his people's land when they were starving because the buffalo had died out. When the situation did not improve, young men in his band grew impatient and attacked villages and Hudson Bay posts during the Northwest Rebellion. Big Bear surrendered to the authorities and was sent to jail for three years.

birth defect: an abnormality that a baby has at birth. It is not caused by the birth but rather by a gene in the baby or an injury that occurred while its organs and tissues were still forming in the mother's womb.

blotting paper: thick, rough paper that is used like a sponge to absorb excess ink on a piece of writing paper when writing with a fountain pen. Blotting paper is pressed down on the ink to prevent it from smudging or running on a page.

British Empire: an old term that referred to Great Britain, all of its dependent countries and provinces, and the British dominions in the world.

British North America: after the American War of Independence (1775-1781), the remaining British colonies, which would one day unite to become Canada, became known as British North America.

British North America (BNA) Act: law passed in 1867 that united the provinces of Canada (Upper and Lower), Nova Scotia and New Brunswick into the self-governing Dominion of Canada. It created the basis of the federal system and laid down the division of powers between federal and provincial governments.

British subject: a citizen of Britain or any of its colonies.

Brown, George (1818–1880): one of the Fathers of Confederation. He joined with Sir John A. Macdonald and others to push for Canadian confederation even while he was leader of the Opposition to Macdonald's ruling party in the Legislative Assembly of the Province of Canada. Another legacy that he left Canada was the Toronto *Globe* (now *Globe and Mail*) newspaper, which he founded in 1844.

Canada: the country formed on July 1, 1867 from the union of Nova Scotia, New Brunswick and the two provinces of Canada (Upper and Lower). Canada eventually grew to include six more provinces and two territories by 1949. In 1999, the territory of Nunavut was created from a part of the Northwest Territories.

Canadian Pacific Railway (CPR) company: the organization formed in 1881 to build a railway from Canada's eastern provinces to British Columbia. The construction of a rail link was one of the conditions for BC's entry into Confederation. Construction took place from 1882 until the last

For additional information on the terms listed in this glossary, consult www.jackfruitpress.com

More words and facts you might want to know.

spike was driven in on November 7, 1885, at Craigellachie, BC. The first passenger train left Montreal on June 28, 1886, and arrived at Port Moody, BC, on July 4. The railway fulfilled its goal of connecting Canada from coast to coast in 1889 when tracks were laid through Maine to Saint John, NB.

Chinese Consolidated Benevolent Association (CCBA): the first community-based Chinese organization in Canada. It was formed in 1884 in Victoria, BC to take care of the sick, poor, and mistreated. The CCBA constitution guaranteed that the unemployed over 60 were eligible for a free trip home to China. The association also ran a home for the sick and poor and paid the burial costs for anyone dying in poverty. As well, the CCBA provided legal aid for those who were unjustly accused of crimes and provided rewards for the capture of people who had killed a Chinese person.

civil war : a war in which different parts of the same country fight each other. The American Civil War (1861-1865) was fought between the northern states of the USA and 11 southern states that wished to separate from the USA. Trouble had been brewing for decades between the two sides because each had strong and opposing views on issues such as slavery, trade and tariffs, and the rights of the states.

Clark, Isabella (1809–1857): first wife of Sir John A. Macdonald. They married in 1843 and had two children: John, who died at the age of 1, and a second son, Hugh John, who went on to become premier of the province of Manitoba.

colonies: settlements of people which are subject to the laws of another country. For example, Upper and Lower Canada were colonies of England.

confederation: the union of a group of states or provinces to form a country.

Conservative Party of Canada: the first party to govern the Dominion of Canada. It began in 1854 when politicians from Upper and Lower Canada joined to form a coalition government of the Province of Canada. It was initially called the Liberal-Conservative Party but changed its name to the Conservative Party when a separate Liberal Party was formed at the time of Confederation. Sir John was its first leader.

constitution: the highest set of laws in a country. Just like you have rules in your home to help take care of your property, relationships, and personal well-being, a constitution is a set of laws or rules that lays out how a government must take care of its people, and the rights these people can expect their government to protect. Most countries have written constitutions that set out the basic laws of their state.

Dominion of Canada: official name of the country of Canada from 1867 to 1949. The title "Dominion" was dropped in 1949 and the country has been known as Canada since then.

Erasmus, George (1949-): president of the Indian Brotherhood of the Northwest Territories and leader of the Assembly of First Nations from 1985 to 1991. He argued that there were three societies in Canada, one of them being First Nations. In 1996 he co-chaired the groundbreaking Royal Commission on Aboriginal Peoples.

Fenian raids (1866, 1870, 1871): attempts to invade Canada carried out by the Fenian Brotherhood (a radical group of Irish immigrants in the United States). In 1866, they invaded along the Niagara and Quebec frontiers. They returned to the United States before Canadian and British reinforcements arrived. For the next several years, the Fenians regrouped and in 1870 they conducted two unsuccessful raids on Quebec again. A final raid in 1871 into Manitoba was also a failure.

First Nations peoples: the descendants of the first inhabitants of North America. The Constitution recognizes three groups of aboriginal people: Indians, Métis and Inuit. These are three separate groups of people with unique heritages, languages, cultural practises and spiritual beliefs.

Governor General: the representative of the king or queen in Canada who provides Royal Assent necessary for all laws passed by Parliament. The Governor General is a figurehead who only performs symbolic formal, ceremonial, and cultural duties, and whose job is to encourage Canadian excellence, identity, unity, and leadership. Governor Generals are Canadian citizens appointed for terms of approximately 5 years. During their term, they live and work in the official residence of Rideau Hall in Ottawa, parts of which are open to the public as a historic site, art gallery, and educational centre.

Gibbs, Mifflin Wistar (1823-1915): Born to a free Black family in Philadelphia, he moved to Victoria in 1858. In addition to serving on the Victoria City Council, he represented Salt Spring Island when British Columbia was deciding whether to join Canada or the USA. He voted to join Canada.

More words and facts you might want to know.

Great Spirit: also known as the Great Creator. Many First Nations people believe that this Being created the world and all living things in it. They believe that the land is for everyone to use and everything has a spirit.

House of Commons: the lower house of Parliament. It consists of a Speaker, the Prime Minister and his Cabinet, members of the governing party, members of the opposition parties, and sometimes a few independent members (elected members who do not belong to an official party). The members of the House (called Members of Parliament or MPs) are elected in constituency elections or by-elections by the Canadian people. The House (often incorrectly referred to as Parliament) is important because it is where all new laws start.

Laurier, Wilfrid: (1841–1911) Canada's 7th Prime Minister and the first one who was a French-Canadian.

Liberal Party of Canada: the second party to govern the Dominion of Canada. The party was formed in 1867 after Canada's Confederation. Canada's 2nd Prime Minister was a Liberal, Sir Alexander Mackenzie.

Lower Canada (1791–1841): province created by the Constitutional Act of 1791, which divided the former Province of Quebec into two parts: Upper Canada and Lower Canada. These two provinces were joined once again to form the Province of Canada in 1841 and were also known as Canada West (Upper Canada or Ontario) and Canada East (Lower Canada or Quebec).

Macdonald, Sir Hugh John (1850–1929): only surviving son of Isabella and Sir John A. Macdonald. Hugh became a lawyer, then a Member of Parliament in Ottawa. He later became Premier of Manitoba, then retired from politics, and returned to practising law. In 1911, he became the police magistrate in Winnipeg. In 1913, he was knighted.

Macdonald, Margaret Mary Theodora (1869–1933): daughter of Sir John A. Macdonald and his second wife, Susan Agnes Bernard. She was affectionately called "Baboo" by her father. She was born with hydrocephalus and was not able to walk or speak clearly. Mary was included in her family's activities and attended Parliament to see and hear her father at work.

Mackenzie, Alexander (1822–1892): 2nd Prime Minister of Canada (1873 –1878) who formed the first Liberal government in the Dominion of Canada. Born in Scotland, he immigrated to Canada in 1842. He worked as a stonemason, a building contractor, and a newspaper editor before entering politics.

Mackenzie, William Lyon (1795–1861): leader of the Upper Canada Rebellion in 1837. First elected to the Legislative Assembly of Upper Canada, he later became the first mayor of Toronto. After an unsuccessful attempt to overthrow the government of Upper Canada, Mackenzie escaped to the USA, where he set up a provisional government.

McGee, Thomas D'Arcy (1825–1868): an Irish-Canadian leader, poet, and politician who was one of the Fathers of Confederation.

manifest destiny: the strong belief held by the United States that it had the right to grab land, unchallenged from the Atlantic all the way to the Pacific, and even beyond. The idea of "Manifest Destiny" was often used by Americans to justify taking over Texas, Oregon, New Mexico, California, Alaska, Hawaii, and the Philippines.

mental illness: a disease that affects the brain. These diseases sometimes really upset people's thinking, feelings, moods, and their ability to relate to others and deal with the demands of everyday life. Mental illness is not the result of personal weakness or lack of "will power." It can be treated with medication and supportive counselling.

Métis: a person whose ancestry is half First Nations and half French Canadian. Métis culture combines both backgrounds.

National Policy: a three-point plan introduced by John A. Macdonald's government in 1878. Macdonald reasoned that a prosperous Canada would be more likely to stay together. His plan included placing high tariffs on imported goods, building a transcontinental railway, and encouraging people to settle in western Canada.

Northwest Rebellion (1885): the second rebellion led by Louis Riel. By the 1880s, European and other settlers were moving into modern-day Saskatchewan and the Métis saw their traditional lifestyle threatened. First Nations People had signed treaties giving up claim to the whole of the territory and agreeing to settle on reserves. The Canadian government, however, did not live up to its end of the deal. The Métis of Saskatchewan invited Louis Riel to help them. He set up a provisional government which was eventually overthrown by Canadian troops. Riel surrendered and was hanged for treason.

For additional information on the terms listed in this glossary, consult www.jackfruitpress.com

Still more words and facts you might want to know.

Pacific Scandal (1872–1873): charges of corruption against Prime Minister John A. Macdonald in awarding the contract to build a transcontinental railroad. It resulted in the downfall of Macdonald's Conservative government and the cancellation of the contract, thus delaying the construction of the railroad for several years.

political party: a group of people who join together because they have the same opinions about how to run a government and try to get into power by being elected by the voting population. In Canada the political party with the greatest number of elected members gets to run the government. At the present time some Canadian parties are: Liberals, Conservatives, and New Democrats, Bloq Québecois and the Green Party.

Poundmaker (1842-1886): a gifted speaker, peacemaker, and Plains Cree chief in what is now central Saskatchewan. Because his people were starving, he insisted the Canadian government promise to supply food and farm tools to his people. When the government did not live up to its promises, his band wanted to join Louis Riel's Métis in their fight against the government but Poundmaker delayed them until the Métis were defeated. He surrendered to Canadian authorities and was sentenced to three years in prison. He was released after one year because of poor health.

primers: elementary school books used to teach children how to read.

provisional government: temporary system of governing put in place until a permanent one is formed.

Queen Victoria (1819–1901): Queen of the United Kingdom of Great Britain and Ireland (1837–1901) and empress of India (1876–1901). She gave her name to an era, the Victorian Age.

Red River Rebellion (1869-70): the events in which the Métis of Red River (modern day Manitoba) took up arms against the Canadian government. The crisis arose because the Hudson's Bay Company had agreed to sell Rupert's Land, which included the Red River area, to Canada. In protest, Louis Riel and other Métis proclaimed a provisional government to negotiate with Canada. Things turned violent when some Canadian settlers took up arms against the Métis. The Canadian government responded by sending troops to enforce federal authority. Riel fled before the expedition arrived and went into exile in the USA. The Canadian government eventually agreed to meet some of the demands of the Métis. The result was the Manitoba Act, which created the province of Manitoba.

Riel, Louis (1844–1885): a Métis lawyer who led two armed rebellions against the Canadian government to defend the rights and lands of the French and First Nations people in the territories that later became Manitoba and Saskatchewan. Riel led the Red River Rebellion in 1869, then went into exile in the USA, fearing for his safety. He later moved to Saskatchewan, where he led the Northwest Rebellion in 1885. This rebellion was quickly crushed and Riel was hanged for treason.

seat in Parliament: place where an elected Member of Parliament sits in the House of Commons, part of Canada's Parliament. Parliament is the national legislature in Canada. It has two houses, an upper house called the Senate, and a lower house called the House of Commons. Senators are appointed by the Governor General but the Canadian people elect their representatives in the House of Commons.

Scott, Thomas (1842-1870): an Irish settler who opposed Riel's provisional government of the Red River settlement (now Winnipeg). He was executed on the orders of Louis Riel on March 4, 1870.

temperance societies: associations of people whose aim is to restrict or outlaw alcohol.

Thompson, Sir John Sparrow David (1845–1894): Canada's 4th Prime Minister. Initially reluctant to enter politics, Thompson became Prime Minister in 1892 after the resignation of John Abbott, Canada's 3rd Prime Minister.

treaty: an official agreement between two groups of people, usually involving land, money or civil rights. Each group promises to do or give something to the other group. When the First Nations people signed treaties with the Canadian government, the First Nations gave some of their land to the government while the government promised a variety of things, like food, money, and homes.

Upper Canada (1791–1841): province created by the Constitutional Act of 1791, which divided the former Province of Quebec into two parts: Upper Canada and Lower Canada. These two provinces were joined once again to form the Province of Canada in 1841 and were also known as Canada West (Upper Canada, or Ontario) and Canada East (Lower Canada, or Quebec).

For additional information on the terms listed in this glossary, consult www.jackfruitpress.com

Index

A
Abbott, John, 43, 47
Alaska, 25, 26, 46
Alberta, 38, 43. *See* Banff
alcoholism, 6, 20, 21, 44
alderman, 14, 41, 44
Allan, Sir Hugh, 28, 29, 44
American War of Independence, 16, 44

B
Banff National Park, 31, 43
bar examination, 13, 44
Bernard, Susan Agnes, 19, 22, 42, 44, 46
Big Bear, 32, 44
blacks in Canada, 28, 36, 37, 41
British Columbia, 5, 16, 25, 28, 33, 38, 42, 44, 45
British Empire, 16, 17, 44
British North America, 8, 10, 14, 16, 17, 25, 40, 41, 44
British North America Act, 13, 17, 42
Brown, George, 20, 22, 42, 44

C
Canada East. *See* Quebec
Canada West. *See* Ontario
Canadian Pacific Railway Company, 25, 26, 28, 29, 31, 32, 33, 37, 40, 41, 43, 44, 45, 46
Cartier, George-Etienne, 41, 42
Charlottetown, 36, 42
China, 33, 41, 43
  immigration to Canada, 33, 43
Chinese Canadians, 33, 43, 45
Chinese Consolidated Benevolent Association, 33, 45
Chinese Head Tax, 33
Chinese Immigration Act, 33
Civil War, 25, 42, 45
Clark, Isabella, 2, 19, 20, 41, 45, 46
colonies, 5, 10, 14, 16, 17, 25, 40, 45
Confederation, 16, 17, 25, 36, 37, 38, 42, 43, 45
Conservative Party of Canada, 14, 29, 31, 35, 41, 42, 45
Constitution, 6, 13, 36, 45

D
Dominion of Canada, 13, 17, 25, 38, 44, 45

E
Education, early days, 11
Erasmus, George, 15, 45

F
Farrar, Edward, 35
Fenian raids, 24, 25, 36, 42, 45
First Nations, 46, 47. *See* Big Bear, Poundmaker, Great Spirit, Erasmus, Métis
Fisheries Treaty, 43
France, 40, 41, 43
Free Trade, 41

G
George IV, 40
Georgia, State of, 19
Gibbs, Mifflin Wistar, 28, 45
Glasgow, 9, 40
Glenora, 9, 10, 40
Governor General, 29, 45
Great Spirit, 15, 46

H
Hay Bay, 10
House of Commons, 5, 7, 18, 22, 35, 42, 46
Hudson's Bay Company, 26, 27, 40
Hydrocephalus, 22, 46

I
Indian Act, 43

K
Kingston, 8, 10, 13, 14, 19, 20, 35, 36, 40, 41

L
Laurier, Wilfrid, 38, 46
Liberal Party of Canada, 29, 35, 38, 46
Liberal-Conservative Party, 42, 45
Lower Canada. *See* Quebec

M
Macdonald, Helen Shaw, 9, 10, 42
Macdonald, Hugh, 9, 10
Macdonald, James, 9, 10, 40
Macdonald, John Jr., 19, 20
Macdonald, Louisa, 9, 19
Macdonald, Margaret, 9, 19
Macdonald, Margaret Mary Theodora, 7, 22, 42, 46
Macdonald, Sir Hugh John, 19, 20, 35, 41, 46
Macdonald, Sir John Alexander
  boarding school, 10
  born, 9
  death, 35
  enemies, 6, 22, 27, 28, 29, 32, 35, 38
  family, 9, 19, 20, 22, 35
  friends, 23
  humour, 6, 7, 14, 18, 38
  knighted, 17
  law practice, 13, 20, 40
  quotations, 10, 18, 22, 29, 35, 39
Mackenzie, Alexander, 29, 31, 43, 46
Mackenzie, George, 13, 40
Mackenzie, William Lyon, 13, 40, 46
Macpherson, Maria, 20
Manifest destiny, 25, 46
Manitoba, 6, 25, 27, 28, 31, 38, 42, 43
McDougall, William, 27
McGee, Thomas D'Arcy, 23, 42, 46
Métis, 26, 27, 28, 31, 32, 35, 37, 40, 46
Mounties. *See* Northwest Mounted Police and Royal Canadian Mounted Police

N
Napanee, 13, 40
National park, first. *See* Banff
National Policy, 31, 46
New Brunswick, 14, 25, 36, 38, 40, 41
Newfoundland, 14, 17, 37, 38
Northwest Company, 40
Northwest Mounted Police, 43
Northwest Rebellion, 6, 31, 43, 46
Northwest Territories, 25, 26, 28, 31, 38, 42, 43
Nova Scotia, 14, 25, 38, 41

O
Ontario, 8, 10, 13, 14, 16, 25, 35, 38, 41, 47
Ottawa, 6, 7, 23, 27, 36, 37, 41

P
Pacific Scandal, 6, 25, 28, 29, 43, 47
Poundmaker, 32
President of the United States, 35, 42
Prince Edward Island, 17, 25, 36, 38, 42, 43
Province of Canada, 13, 14, 41
Provisional Government, 27, 47

Q
Quebec, 6, 8, 11, 14, 16, 25, 27, 32, 38, 40, 46
Quebec City, 8, 16
Queen Victoria, 17, 25, 47

R
Red River Rebellion, 6, 25, 47
Riel, Louis, 6, 25, 26, 27, 28, 31, 32, 35, 42, 43, 47
Royal Canadian Mounted Police, 6
Russia, 25

S
Saskatchewan, 31, 38
Scandal. *See* Pacific Scandal
Schools
  Early Canadian, 11
Scotland, 9, 10, 19, 40, 41
Scott, Thomas, 27, 32, 42
Seat in Parliament, 14, 47
Slavery, 28, 36, 40, 41, 42, 45
Surveyors, 27

T
Tax, 31, 33, 43
Temperance Societies, 21, 47
Thompson, Sir John, 5, 47
Toronto Globe, 18, 20
Treason, 32, 35
Treaty, 15, 41, 42, 43, 47

U
United States of America, 5, 14, 16, 19, 20, 24, 25, 26, 27, 28, 35, 40, 41
Upper Canada. *See* Ontario
Upper Canada Rebellion, 13, 40

W
Washington, D.C., 42

Y
Yukon, 38